homemade
cooking

simply delicious family meals

First published in 2011

Parragon
Queen Street House
4 Queen Street
Bath
BA1 1HE UK

Copyright Parragon books Ltd 2011

ISBN: 978-1-4454-4050-7

Printed in China

The times given are an approximate guide only.
Preparation times differ according to the techniques used
by different people and the cooking times may also vary
from those given as a result of the type of oven used.
Optional ingredients, variations or serving suggestions
have not been included in the calculations.

Recipes using raw or very lightly cooked eggs should
be avoided by infants, the elderly, pregnant women
convalescents and anyone with a chronic condition.
Pregnant and breast-feeding women are advised to
avoid eating peanuts and peanut products. People with
nut allergies should be aware that some of the prepared
ingredients used in this book may contain nuts. Always
check the photography before use.

contents

introduction

American cooking is distinguished by its regional variety and by its contributions of homemade recipes from generations of creative cooks. In *Homemade Cooking* the recipes reflect our unique culinary history, with a focus on much-loved comfort-food classics.

Included are suggestions for every occasion, from mouthwatering breakfasts and brunches (*Sausage and Mushroom Breakfast Casserole, Corned Beef Hash, Potato Pancakes with Smoked Salmon and Dill Sour Cream*) to all-time favorite appetizers and snacks, (*Deviled Eggs* and *Crispy Chicken Fingers*), to delightful cookies and treats, (classic *Double Fudge Brownies* and *Carrot Cake*). The heart of the book are the main meals, from *Spaghetti and Meatballs* and *Braised Short Ribs* to a fresh way to prepare *Roast Turkey Breast* and *All American Meatloaf.*

Every region is represented, from *Buffalo Chicken Wings* to *Maryland Crab Cakes* and *New Orleans-Style French Toast*. Ethnic favorites abound, from a Mexican-inspired *Chorizo and Cheese Quesadillas with Chipotle Sour Cream* to Italian-style *Chicken Parmesan Casserole*. And, of course, old-fashioned home cooking is front and center, from *Mom's Chicken Noodle Soup*, to classic *New York Strip Steak* and buttery *Buttermilk Biscuits*.

With a host of easy-to-make, delectable recipes and beautiful photographs illustrating each and every recipe, this is a cookbook every home cook will want on her shelf and will turn to—and cook from— for decades.

simple appetizers and snacks

deviled eggs

Deviled eggs are a kitschy party food favorite. They're fun to make, fun to serve, fun to eat, and even fun to make fun of. It's not a party until a plate of deviled eggs shows up.

makes 24

12 large eggs

1 teaspoon white wine vinegar

4 tablespoons mayonnaise

½ teaspoon Dijon mustard

½ teaspoon prepared horseradish

¼ teaspoon Worcestershire sauce

½ teaspoon salt

Dash of Tabasco

Pinch of cayenne pepper

Paprika or more cayenne pepper to garnish

1 tablespoon thinly sliced chives

Place the eggs in a single layer in a large saucepan and cover with cold water by one inch. Bring the water to a boil over high heat. Turn off the heat, and cover tightly with the lid, and set a timer for 17 minutes.

Carefully pour off most the hot water, and fill the pan with cold water. Allow to sit for 3 minutes. Pour off most of the water, and again fill the pan with cold water. Leave for 15 minutes. Drain and refrigerate the eggs until needed.

Peel the eggs under cold running water. Cut the eggs in half lengthwise and pop out the yolks into a small mixing bowl. Add the vinegar, mayonnaise, mustard, horseradish, Worcestershire, salt, Tabasco, and cayenne. Mash and mix with a wire whisk until smooth and light.

Using a spoon, or pastry bag with a star tip, fill the egg white halves with the yolk mixture. Sprinkle tops with paprika or cayenne pepper. Chill before serving with the sliced chives.

maryland crab cakes with tartar sauce

The main ingredient in perfect crab cakes should be...crab! The last thing you want is the taste of filler getting in the way of the flavor of fresh crab.

makes 6

1 large egg, beaten
2 tbs mayonnaise
½ tsp Dijon mustard
¼ tsp Worcestershire sauce
½ tsp Old Bay seasoning
¼ tsp salt, or to taste
Pinch of cayenne pepper
1 pound fresh lump crabmeat, well drained
10 saltine crackers
Plain breadcrumbs
1 tbs vegetable oil
2 tbs unsalted butter

For the tartar sauce
1 cup mayonnaise
¼ cup sweet pickle relish
1 tbs finely minced onion
1 tbs chopped capers
1 tbs chopped parsley
1½ tbs freshly squeezed lemon juice
Dash of Worcestershire sauce
Few drops of Tabasco
Salt and freshly ground black pepper to taste

Whisk together the egg, mayonnaise, mustard, Worcestershire, Old Bay, salt, and cayenne to a mixing bowl. Crush the crackers into very fine crumbs and add to the bowl. Stir until combined. Let sit for 5 minutes.

Gently fold in the crabmeat. Cover the bowl and refrigerate for at least 1 hour.

Sprinkle the breadcrumbs lightly over a large plate. Shape the crab mixture into 6 cakes, and place on the plate. Dust the tops of each crab cake lightly with more breadcrumbs. These cakes are almost all crab, which makes them fragile. They will bind together as the egg cooks, and golden-brown crust forms.

Heat the vegetable oil and butter in a large skillet over medium-high heat. When the foam from the butter begins to dissipate, carefully transfer each crab cake to the pan. Sauté until golden brown, about 4 minutes per side. Drain on a paper towel, and serve with the sauce.

For the sauce: Mix together all the ingredients in a bowl. Refrigerate at least an hour before serving. Makes 1½ cups.

buffalo chicken wings

Everyone's favorite appetizer is usually deep fried, but this delicious home version uses a very hot oven instead.

makes 40

4 pounds chicken wings

1 tablespoon vegetable oil

1 tablespoon all-purpose flour

1 teaspoon salt

For the sauce

²/₃ cup hot sauce

½ cup (1 stick) cold unsalted butter, cut into 1-inch slices

1½ tablespoons white vinegar

¼ teaspoon Worcestershire sauce

1 teaspoon Tabasco

¼ teaspoon cayenne pepper

a pinch of garlic powder

Salt

Preheat oven to 425°F. If the chicken wings being used were frozen and thawed, be sure they're completely dry before starting recipe. If using whole wings, cut each into two pieces (in wing-speak called the "flat" and the "drum"). The small wing tips can be discarded, or saved for stock. In a large mixing bowl, toss the wings with the oil, flour, and salt until evenly coated.

Line two heavy-duty baking sheets with lightly greased foil or silicon baking mats. Divide the wings and spread out evenly. Do not crowd. Bake for 25 minutes, remove, and turn the wings over. Return to the oven and cook another 20 to 30 minutes, or until the wings are well-browned and cooked through.

Note: Cooking times will vary based on size of the wings. When fully cooked, the bones will easily pull out from the meat.

While the wings are baking, mix all the sauce ingredients in a saucepan. Bring to a simmer, whisking, over medium heat. Remove from heat and reserve. Taste sauce; adjust for salt and spiciness, if desired.

After the wings are cooked, transfer to a large mixing bowl. Pour the warm sauce over the hot wings and toss with a spoon or spatula to completely coat.

hot spinach and artichoke dip

This warm, savory dip is fast to make, and a proven crowd-pleaser. Great with chips, but even better on slices of fresh French bread.

serves 8

2 tablespoons butter

½ cup chopped scallions, white and light green parts only

Pinch of salt

2 cloves garlic, finely minced

1 package (10 ounces) frozen chopped spinach, thawed, drained, squeezed dry

1 (14 ounce) can artichoke hearts, drained, roughly chopped

8 ounces (1 cup) cream cheese

¼ cup sour cream

¼ teaspoon hot sauce

Small pinch of nutmeg

½ cup (2 ounces) grated Parmesan cheese, preferably Parmigiano Reggiano

¼ cup (1 ounce) grated mozzarella cheese

Preheat oven to 400°F. Sauté the onions with a pinch of salt in the butter over medium heat until translucent. Add the garlic, stir to combine, and immediately turn off the heat; reserve.

In a mixing bowl, combine the spinach, artichoke hearts, cream cheese, sour cream, hot sauce, nutmeg, and Parmesan cheese. Add the onion mixture, and stir until thoroughly mixed.

Transfer the mixture into a small baking dish, and top with the mozzarella cheese. Bake until bubbling and golden, about 25 minutes. The dip may be placed under a hot broiler for a few minutes, if a browner top is desired.

chorizo and cheese quesadillas with chipotle sour cream

Quesadillas are such a great party food – fast, easy, and a proven crowd-pleaser.

serves 4

1 cup (4 ounces) grated mozzarella

1 cup (4 ounces) grated cheddar cheese

8 ounces chorizo sausage (outer case removed) or ham diced

4 scallions, finely chopped

2 fresh green chilies seeded, chopped

8 flour tortillas

Vegetable oil for brushing

Salt and pepper to taste

Lime wedges to garnish

For the sauce

1 cup sour cream

1 tablespoon minced canned chipotles in adobo sauce or ¾ teaspoon chipotle powder

Place the cheeses, chorizo, scallions, chilies, salt, and pepper in a bowl and mix together.

Divide the mixture among 4 of the flour tortillas, then top with the remaining tortillas.

Brush a large, nonstick or heavy-bottom skillet with oil and heat over medium heat. Add 1 quesadilla and cook, pressing it down with a spatula, for 4 to 5 minutes until the underside is crisp and lightly browned. Turn over and cook the other side until the cheese is melting. Remove from the skillet and keep warm. Cook the remaining quesadillas.

Cut each one into quarters, arrange on a warmed serving plate, and serve immediately accompanied by some guacamole, salsa, and sour cream sauce.

To make the sour cream sauce: In a medium bowl, combine the sour cream and chipotles. Whisk together to fully incorporate.

crispy chicken fingers with honey mustard dip

Millions of kids can't be wrong – crispy chicken fingers rule! Make a batch of these and see what a certain "nugget" of chicken is really supposed to taste like.

serves 8

1 cup all-purpose flour

2 teaspoons salt

1 teaspoon garlic salt

1 teaspoon chipotle pepper

½ teaspoon white pepper

4 large skinless, boneless chicken breasts, cut into ½-inch strips

4 eggs, beaten

1 tablespoon milk

3 cups Japanese-style panko bread crumbs

Vegetable oil for frying

For the dip

½ cup mayonnaise

2 tablespoons Dijon mustard

2 tablespoons yellow mustard

1 tablespoon rice vinegar

2 tablespoons honey

½ teaspoon hot sauce, optional

Combine the flour, salt, garlic salt, chipotle, and white pepper in a large, sealable plastic freezer bag. Shake to mix. Add the chicken strips, seal the bag, and shake vigorously to coat evenly.

In a mixing bowl, whisk together the eggs and milk. Add the chicken strips, shaking off the excess flour as you remove them from the bag. Stir until the strips are completely coated in the egg mixture.

Pour the breadcrumbs in a shallow pan. Use one hand (called the "wet" hand) to remove the chicken strips from the bowl of eggs, a few at a time, allowing the excess egg to drip off, and place in the pan of panko. Use the other hand (called the "dry" hand) to coat the chicken in the breadcrumbs, pressing them in firmly. As they are breaded, place the strips on baking sheets or racks. When done breading, let the chicken strips rest for 10 to 15 minutes before frying.

Pour about ½ inch of oil in a large, heavy skillet (ideally cast iron) and set over medium-high heat. When the oil is hot enough to fry (350°F to 375°F or test with a small piece of breading), cook for 2 to 3 minutes per side, or until golden brown and cooked through. Work in batches; drain on paper towels or baking racks, and keep the cooked chicken fingers in a warm oven (175°F) until all are done.

To make the honey mustard dip: Combine all the ingredients and mix well. Serve immediately.

mom's chicken noodle soup

There's a popular book entitled *Chicken Soup for the Soul*.
This really is chicken soup for the soul.

serves 6

For the broth

1 large whole chicken, about 4 to 5 pounds

Salt and freshly ground black pepper to taste

1 carrot, chopped

1 rib celery, chopped

1 onion, chopped

1 clove garlic, peeled

4 sprigs thyme

1 bay leaf

1 whole clove

1 teaspoon ketchup

For the soup

1 tablespoon butter

1 onion, diced

1 cup diced carrots

1 cup diced celery

¼ teaspoon poultry seasoning

2 cups uncooked egg noodles, or other macaroni

1 tablespoon chopped parsley

Preheat oven to 450°F. Season the chicken inside and out with salt and pepper. Add the carrots, celery and onions to an oiled 9 x 13-inch roasting pan, and place the chicken on top. Roast for 60 minutes, or until a thermometer inserted in the thickest part of a thigh registers 160°F.

Remove the chicken from the oven and allow to rest until cool enough to handle. Pull off the breast meat, and larger pieces of thigh and leg meat, and refrigerate until needed.

Transfer the chicken carcass and vegetables from the roasting pan into a large stockpot. Add 2 quarts of cold water, along with the garlic, thyme, bay leaf, clove, and ketchup. Bring to a boil, turn the heat to low, and simmer for 2 hours. Every so often, add a splash of water to the pot so the liquid level remains the same.

While the broth is simmering, place a soup pot on medium-low heat. Melt the butter and sauté the diced onion, carrots, and celery in the butter until they begin to soften, about 15 minutes. Stir in the poultry seasoning, turn off the heat, and reserve until the broth is done.

Skim the fat from the top of the broth, and strain it into the soup pot with the sautéed vegetables; bring to a boil. Turn to low and simmer until the vegetables are tender. Taste, and add salt and fresh ground black pepper to taste. Turn heat up to high, add the egg noodles and boil for 7 minutes. Dice the chicken and add to the pot. Turn heat to medium and simmer until the noodles are tender. Stir in the parsley, and serve.

garden vegetable soup

This recipe is great as is, but if you're in the mood for something more substantial, you can add some macaroni for a quick and delicious minestrone, or toss in some leftover roast chicken for an even heartier soup.

serves 6

2 tablespoons olive oil

1 yellow onion, diced

2 ribs celery, sliced into ¼ inch pieces

3 carrots, peeled, cut into ½ inch pieces

2 cloves garlic, finely minced

6 cups chicken or vegetable broth

¼ teaspoon dried thyme

¼ teaspoon dried basil

2 cups cubed zucchini

1 cup corn kernels

1 (15-ounce) can navy beans, drained, rinsed

1 cup cherry tomato halves

1 large handful baby spinach leaves

¼ cup chopped fresh Italian parsley leaves

Salt and fresh ground black pepper

Heat the olive oil in a soup pot over medium-low heat. Add the onions, celery, carrots, and garlic. Cook, stirring occasionally, until they begin to soften, about 10 minutes.

Add the broth, thyme, and basil; turn up heat to high, and bring to a simmer. Turn down to medium-low and cook for 10 minutes. Add the zucchini, corn, and navy beans. Cover and simmer for 15 minutes, or until the vegetables are tender.

Add the tomatoes, spinach, and parsley. As soon as the spinach wilts, turn off the heat. Season with salt and fresh ground black pepper to taste.

Serve immediately.

deli-style macaroni salad

Take your time, and use your sharpest knife to get a nice fine dice on the veggies in this classic pasta salad. When made right, this is a macaroni salad where every forkful bursts with flavor.

serves 8

1 pound dry elbow macaroni, cooked, rinsed in cold water, and drained well

For the dressing

1½ cups mayonnaise

½ cup sour cream

2 tablespoons cider vinegar

1 tablespoon Dijon mustard

1 teaspoon sugar

½ cup finely diced celery

¼ cup minced red onion

½ cup sweet pickle relish

¼ finely grated carrot

2 tablespoons seeded and finely diced red bell pepper

¼ cup chopped parsley

½ teaspoon freshly ground black pepper

1½ teaspoons salt, or to taste

Whisk together all the dressing ingredients in a large mixing bowl, and add the drained pasta. Toss to combine thoroughly. Refrigerate for at least 2 hours before serving.

Note: Some of the vegetables can be reserved to scatter over the top for a more colorful presentation.

breakfast and brunch

buttermilk biscuits

Making buttermilk biscuits would be the first event in any food decathlon. Anyone can make them, but to get great biscuits it helps to have a gentle and intuitive disposition. Use a light touch because over-mixing will toughen the dough.

makes 12-14

2 cups all-purpose flour

2 teaspoons baking powder

¼ teaspoon baking soda

1 teaspoon salt

7 tablespoons unsalted butter, cut into thin slices, chilled in freezer

¾ cup cold buttermilk

Preheat oven to 425°F. In a mixing bowl, whisk together the dry ingredients to thoroughly combine. Cut in the ice cold butter slices using a wire pastry blender, until the mixture has the texture of coarse crumbs.

Make a well in the center and pour in the cold buttermilk. Stir the dry ingredients into the buttermilk with a fork until a loose, sticky dough is formed. Stop as soon as the mixture comes together. Form into a ball and turn the dough out onto a floured work surface.

With floured hands, pat the dough into a rectangle (about 8x4-inch-thick). Fold dough in thirds (like folding a letter-sized piece of paper). Repeat this process twice more.

On a lightly-floured surface, roll or pat the dough out about ½-inch thick. Cut with a round biscuit cutter, and place on a parchment or silicon mat-lined baking sheet, a few inches apart. You can gather up any extra dough after cutting, and repeat to get a few more biscuits, although the texture may suffer from the extra working.

Make a slight depression in the center of each biscuit with your thumb (to help them rise evenly). Brush the tops lightly with buttermilk. Bake for about 15 minutes, or until risen and golden brown. Cool on a rack for 10 minutes before serving.

corned beef hash

To say that fresh, crusty homemade corned beef hash is superior to that pink paste from the can may be the biggest culinary understatement of all time.

serves 6

2 tablespoons butter

1 tablespoon vegetable oil

1½ lbs cooked corned beef, cut in small cubes

½ cup diced onions

1½ lbs white potatoes, peeled, cut in small cubes

Salt and freshly ground black pepper to taste

¼ teaspoon paprika

¼ teaspoon garlic powder

¼ cup seeded and diced green bell pepper, or jalapeño pepper if a spicier version is desired

2 tablespoons prepared roasted tomato salsa

1 tablespoon freshly chopped chives

Add the butter, oil, corned beef, and onions to a large, cold, nonstick or well-seasoned cast iron skillet. Turn heat to medium-low and cook, stirring occasionally, while you prepare the potatoes.

In a saucepan, boil the potatoes in salted water for about 5 to 7 minutes (depending on the size), until partially cooked, but still very firm. Drain very well and add to the skillet along with the rest of the ingredients.

Mix all the ingredients together thoroughly and press down slightly with a spatula to flatten. Turn up the heat to medium. Every 10 minutes or so, turn the mixture over with a spatula. Do this several times until the mixture is well-browned on both sides. Take your time – the only real secret to great corned beef hash is to make sure it cooks long enough, so the potatoes are crisp-edged, and the cubes of meat get nicely caramelized.

Taste for salt and pepper, and adjust if necessary. Transfer to plates. Top with poached eggs and garnish with freshly chopped chives, if desired.

potato pancakes with smoked salmon and dill sour cream

The secret to great potato pancakes is to make sure you squeeze out all the water before mixing. This will give you beautifully browned, crispy cakes. By the way, if you're out of smoked salmon, these are wonderful with applesauce.

makes 8

2¼ pounds Idaho potatoes, peeled

½ yellow onion, peeled

2 large eggs

3 tablespoons all-purpose flour

1 teaspoon salt

½ teaspoon freshly ground black pepper

Pinch of cayenne pepper

Vegetable oil, as needed

3 to 4 ounces thinly sliced smoked salmon

4 tablespoons sour cream

¼ cup fresh dill, chopped

Using a grater, shred the potatoes, and transfer into a large bowl of cold water. Grate the onion and add to bowl. Let sit for 20 minutes. To another bowl, add the eggs, flour, salt, pepper, and cayenne pepper, and whisk until smooth; reserve.

Drain the potato mixture into a colander, pressing down to squeeze out as much water as possible. Line a baking sheet with several layers of paper towels. Take a handful of the potato mixture, and squeeze hard to extract even more water. Place the "dry" potatoes on the paper towels. Repeat until all the potato mixture has been squeezed dry. Add the potato mixture to the egg mixture, and combine thoroughly.

Pour ¼ inch of vegetable oil into a large, heavy skillet (preferably nonstick). Place over medium-high heat, and when the oil is hot (the surface will begin to shimmer), spoon about ⅓ cup of the potato mixture into the pan, shape into a round, and flatten to about ½ inch thick. Turn down the heat to medium, and fry the pancakes for about 5 minutes per side, or until browned and crispy. You can probably fry 4 pancakes at a time. Drain on paper towels and reserve in a warm oven. To serve, top with the sliced smoked salmon, a dollop of sour cream, the fresh dill, and a few grinds of black pepper.

baked spinach and feta omelet

You could use frozen, but with large bags of fresh, pre-washed and picked spinach so readily available in stores, why would you?

serves 6

1 pound fresh spinach leaves, washed

1 tablespoon butter

6 slices bacon, cut in ¼-inch pieces

½ onion, diced

12 eggs, beaten

Salt and freshly ground black pepper to taste

Pinch of cayenne pepper

½ cup (3-4 ounces) crumbled feta cheese

Preheat oven to 350°F. Put a large stockpot over high heat. Add the butter, and as soon as it melts, dump in all the spinach and cover the pot quickly. Leave for one minute, uncover, and continue cooking, stirring the spinach with a long wooden spoon until just wilted. Transfer to a colander to drain. When the spinach is cool enough to handle, squeeze as much liquid out as possible, and roughly chop. Reserve until needed.

In a 10- to 12-inch ovenproof skillet, cook the bacon over medium heat until almost crisp, add the onions and a pinch of salt, and continue cooking until the onions are translucent, 6 to 7 minutes. Any excess bacon fat can be removed at this point.

Stir in the spinach. Season with salt, freshly ground black pepper, and cayenne to taste. When the spinach is heated through, add the eggs and stir with a spatula to combine thoroughly. Turn off the heat, and top with the crumbled feta cheese. Use the spatula to press the cheese down into the egg slightly.

Bake for 10 minutes, then finish under the broiler for about 3 minutes, or until the eggs are just set, and the top is lightly browned. Let rest for 5 to 10 minutes before slicing and serving.

new orleans-style french toast

This recipe was born as a deliciously decadent solution
for what to do with stale loaves!

serves 4-6

5 large eggs

1 cup milk

½ cup cream

Pinch of salt

1 tablespoon sugar

2 teaspoons vanilla extract

½ teaspoon cinnamon

⅛ teaspoon allspice

12 thick slices day-old French bread (use a regular-sized loaf, not the skinny baguette type)

6 tablespoons butter, plus more as needed

Preheat oven to 375°F. In a large mixing bowl, whisk together the eggs, milk, cream, salt, sugar, vanilla extract, cinnamon, and allspice. Soak the bread slices in the custard mixture for at least 20 minutes, or until completely saturated.

In a large nonstick skillet, lightly brown the slices in batches, in a few tablespoons of butter over medium heat; about 2 minutes per side. Don't cook too dark, as additional browning will occur in the oven.

Transfer to lightly buttered, foil-lined sheet pans, and bake for 10 minutes. After 10 minutes, remove, and turn each slice over. Put back in the oven for another 10 to 15 minutes, or until browned and the bread springs back slightly when tested with a finger.

Serve immediately.

blueberry pancakes

When it's summer in Maine, the state's blueberries feature at every meal, starting with breakfast, when they flavor muffins and pancakes. For a complete New England breakfast, serve these with Vermont maple syrup.

makes 10-12 pancakes

1 cup all-purpose flour

2 tablespoons sugar

2 teaspoons baking powder

½ teaspoon salt

1 cup buttermilk

3 tablespoons butter, melted

1 large egg

1 cup (5 ounces) blueberries, rinsed and patted dry

To serve

Butter

Warm maple syrup

Preheat oven to 275°F. Sift the flour, sugar, baking powder, and salt together into a large bowl and make a well in the center.

Beat the buttermilk, butter, and egg together in a separate small bowl, then pour the mixture into the well in the dry ingredients. Beat the dry ingredients into the liquid, gradually drawing them in from the side, until a smooth batter forms. Gently stir in the blueberries.

Heat a large skillet over medium-high heat until a splash of water dances on the surface. Use a pastry brush or crumpled piece of paper towel and the oil to lightly grease the base of the skillet.

Use a ladle to drop about 4 tablespoons of batter into the skillet and spread it out into a 4-inch round. Continue adding as many pancakes as will fit in your skillet. Leave the pancakes to cook until small bubbles appear on the surface, then flip them over and cook for a further 1 to 2 minutes until the bottoms are golden brown.

Transfer the pancakes to a warmed plate and keep warm in the oven while you cook the remaining pancakes, lightly greasing the skillet for each batch. Serve with a pat of butter on top of each pancake and warm maple syrup for pouring over.

eggs benedict

This dish is the undisputed king of brunch dishes. The trick here is poaching the eggs ahead so you can assemble all the plates at the same time.

serves 6

12 fresh large eggs
1 tablespoon white vinegar
Salt
6 English muffins
Butter as needed
12 slices Canadian bacon

For the hollandaise
1 cup (2 sticks) unsalted butter
5 large egg yolks
2 tablespoons fresh lemon juice
Cayenne pepper to taste
Salt to taste

To prepare the eggs: Working in small batches, poach eggs in a saucepan of very gently simmering salted water to which a tablespoon of white vinegar has been added. As they're done carefully set them into a bowl of cool water. Reserve.

To make the hollandaise: Melt the butter in a small saucepan, and reserve over very low heat until needed. Add the egg yolks and lemon juice to a medium stainless steel bowl. Place over a saucepan with 2 inches of gently simmering water. (Note: the bowl should not be touching the water). Whisk constantly until the mixture thickens and is very warm to the touch.

Remove from the heat and very slowly drizzle in the hot melted butter, whisking constantly until it's all incorporated. The mixture can be thinned with a tablespoon of hot water if desired. Whisk in the cayenne and salt to taste. Cover with foil and keep in a warm spot until needed.

To complete the plates: Bring a large deep skillet filled with 3 inches of salted water to a simmer. Place the English muffin halves on a baking sheet and toast under the broiler until golden, then brush with butter. Place one slice of Canadian bacon on each muffin half.

Transfer the poached eggs into the simmer water until heated through but still soft. Remove eggs with a slotted spoon, and place one on each muffin half. Spoon over the warm hollandaise and serve immediately.

sausage and mushroom breakfast casserole

This hearty breakfast casserole is great hot, but can also be served at room temperature. Be sure to check the fridge before making this, since it's a great way to use up leftover produce. Hey, isn't that a bell pepper in the back of the vegetable drawer?

serves 6-8

1½ pounds potatoes, peeled, cut into 1-inch chunks

2 tablespoons butter

2 cups (1 pound) shredded cheddar cheese

3 cups (1 pound) sweet or hot Italian sausage (or sausage of your choice), casings removed

1 bunch scallions, chopped

1 pound (about 3 cups sliced) button mushrooms

14 eggs, beaten

¼ cup milk

1½ teaspoon salt

½ teaspoon freshly ground black pepper

Dash of Tabasco, optional

Preheat oven to 300°F. Boil the potatoes in salted water until just tender, and drain well. Grease a 13 x 9-inch baking dish with 1 tablespoon butter, and add the potatoes. Top with half the cheese.

Brown the sausage in a skillet over medium heat, breaking it into small pieces with a spatula or wooden spoon as it cooks. When browned, add the scallions and cook for 2 minutes more. Use a slotted spoon to transfer the sausage and scallions into the baking dish.

Pour off any excess grease from the pan, and add 1 table-spoon butter and mushrooms. Add a pinch of salt and cook, stirring, over high heat until well-browned. Add mushrooms to the baking dish and distribute evenly.

Whisk together the eggs, milk, salt, freshly ground black pepper, and Tabasco in a mixing bowl. Pour over the sausage and mushrooms. Give the baking dish a jiggle or two, to make sure the eggs are distributed. Top with the rest of the cheese.

Bake for about 35 minutes, or until just set. If desired, place under a hot broiler for a minute or two to brown the top. Let rest at least 15 minutes before serving. Serve hot or at room temperature.

banana nut bread

Next time those bananas are looking a little past their prime, remember this great nutty loaf.

serves 6

2 cups all-purpose flour

1 teaspoon salt

1 teaspoon baking powder

1 teaspoon baking soda

½ cup (1 stick) unsalted butter, softened

1 cup sugar

2 large eggs

1½ cups mashed banana (usually 3 bananas is perfect)

1 cup chopped walnuts

2 tablespoons milk

Preheat oven to 325°F. Whisk together the flour, salt, baking powder, and baking soda in a mixing bowl for one minute; reserve until needed.

Cream the butter and sugar together until light and fluffy. Beat in the eggs one at a time, mixing thoroughly before adding the next. Mix in the bananas, walnuts, and milk until combined. Add the flour mixture, stirring just until combined.

Pour batter into a buttered and lightly-floured 9 x 5-inch loaf pan. Bake for about 1 hour and 10 minutes, or until a tester inserted in the center comes out clean. Let cool 20 minutes before removing from the pan.

home
made main
meals

firehouse chili con carne

Is this called firehouse chili because it's the kind of hearty dish firemen love, or because of its spicy seasoning? Trick question; it's both!

serves 6

1 tablespoon vegetable oil

1 large yellow onion, diced

2½ lbs lean ground beef

3 cloves garlic, minced

¼ cup chile powder

1 tablespoon ground cumin

1 teaspoon freshly ground black pepper

½ teaspoon chipotle pepper

¼ teaspoon cayenne pepper

1 teaspoon dried oregano

1 teaspoon sugar

1 large green bell pepper, seeded and diced

1 large red bell pepper, seeded and diced

1 (15 ounce) can tomato sauce

2 tablespoons tomato paste

3 cups water, or more as needed

1 (15 ounce) can pinto beans, drained, not rinsed

1 (15 ounce) can kidney beans, drained, not rinsed

Add the vegetable oil and onions to a Dutch oven or other heavy pot. Place over medium-high heat and sauté for about 5 minutes, or until the onions begin to soften. Add the ground beef, and cook for about 10 minutes. As the beef browns, use a wooden spoon to break the meat into very small pieces.

Add the garlic, chili powder, ground cumin, black pepper, chipotle pepper, cayenne pepper, oregano, and sugar. Cook, stirring, for 2 minutes.

Stir in the bell peppers, tomato sauce, tomato paste, and water. Bring up to a simmer; reduce the heat to medium-low and cook, uncovered, stirring occasionally for 60 minutes.

After 60 minutes, stir in the beans and simmer for another 30 minutes. If needed, add more water anytime during the cooking to adjust desired thickness. Taste for salt and pepper, and adjust. Serve hot, garnished with sour cream, grated pepper jack, and fresh cilantro leaves, as desired.

braised beef short ribs

This is one of those recipes that will warm
you from the inside out.

serves 6

3½ pounds (8 pieces) beef short ribs

Salt and freshly ground black pepper

4 slices bacon, cut in ½ inch pieces

1 large onion, diced

1 rib celery, diced

4 cloves garlic, minced

2 tablespoons flour

1 cup dry sherry wine

3 cups beef broth, or veal stock if available

6 springs fresh thyme

1 bay leaf

2 teaspoon tomato paste

Preheat oven to 350°F. Add the bacon to a heavy Dutch oven and fry over a medium heat on the stove top until the fat is rendered out. Remove the bacon with a slotted spoon and reserve, leaving the fat in the pan.

Turn the stove heat up to medium-high, and brown the short ribs very well on all sides. Remove the short ribs and reserve. Add the onions and celery; reduce the heat to medium, and sauté for about 5 minutes, until the onions soften.

Add the garlic and flour; cook, stirring, for 2 minutes. Whisk in the sherry (by the way, don't even think of using cooking sherry); turn heat up to high, and bring to a boil, scraping off any browned bits. Add the beef broth, tomato paste, thyme, bay leaf, beef short ribs, and ½ teaspoon of salt.

When the liquid returns to a simmer, cover tightly, and place in the oven. Braise for 2 hours, or until the meat is fork tender. Skim any excess fat from the top. Taste and adjust the seasoning. Serve the short ribs with the sauce spooned over.

all-american meatloaf

Many consider meatloaf and mashed potatoes to be the quintessential comfort food. This modern version uses lots of aromatic vegetables to add moisture and flavor.

serves 6-8

3 cloves garlic, peeled

½ cup diced carrot

½ cup diced celery

½ cup diced yellow onion

½ cup diced red bell pepper, fresh or jarred

4 large white mushrooms, sliced

1 tablespoon olive oil

2 tablespoons butter

1 teaspoon dried thyme

2 teaspoons finely minced fresh rosemary

1 teaspoon Worcestershire sauce

¼ cup ketchup

½ teaspoon cayenne pepper

2½ pounds ground chuck

2 teaspoons salt

1 teaspoon black pepper

2 eggs, beaten

1 cup plain bread crumbs

For the glaze

2 tablespoons brown sugar

2 tablespoons ketchup

1 tablespoon Dijon mustard

Pinch of salt

Preheat oven to 325°F. Add the garlic, carrot, celery, onion, red bell pepper, and white mushrooms into a food processor. Pulse until the vegetables are finely minced.

Melt the butter and olive oil in a large skillet over medium heat; add the vegetable mixture and cook, stirring, about 10 minutes. The vegetables are done when the mixture is lightly caramelized. Remove from the heat and stir in the thyme, rosemary, Worcestershire, ketchup, and cayenne pepper. Set aside and let cool.

Add the ground beef to a large mixing bowl. Pour in the cooled vegetable mixture, salt, pepper, and eggs. Gently combine the mixture with your fingers; add the breadcrumbs and continue mixing until combined.

Lightly grease a shallow roasting pan. Place the meatloaf in the center, and form into a loaf shape, about 6- by 4-inches. Place the meatloaf in the center of the preheated oven and bake for 30 minutes.

To make the glaze: Whisk together the brown sugar, ketchup, Dijon, and pinch of salt in a small bowl. After 30 minutes, remove the meatloaf and evenly spread the glaze over the top and down the sides.

Return to the oven and continue baking for another 35 to 45 minutes, or until you reach an internal temperature of 155 °F. Let rest for at least 15 minutes before serving.

new york strip steak and mushrooms

Pan-seared strip steaks with sautéed mushrooms is a classic combination. The secret to bringing out the earthy goodness of the mushrooms is to make sure they're thoroughly browned before finishing the salad.

serves 4

For the mushroom salad

2 tablespoons butter

¼ cup olive oil

6 cups (2 pounds) thickly sliced large button mushrooms

2 garlic cloves, minced

3 tablespoons sherry vinegar

1 tablespoon freshly chopped tarragon

Salt and freshly ground black pepper to taste

For the steaks

4 (10-ounce) thick-cut New York strip steaks

Salt and coarsely-ground black pepper to taste

1 tablespoon vegetable oil

¼ cup chicken broth

1 tablespoon cold butter

Melt the butter and the olive oil, in a large frying pan, over medium-high heat. When the butter starts to sizzle, add the mushrooms and cook, stirring, for 10 to 15 minutes, or until the mushroom juices have evaporated, and they're very well browned. Stir in the garlic, and cook for 2 minutes.

Pour in the vinegar, and as soon as it starts to boil, turn off the heat. Transfer the mixture to a bowl, and allow to cool to room temperature. Add the tarragon, salt, and freshly ground black pepper to taste. Reserve until needed.

Season the steaks generously on both sides with salt and coarsely-ground black pepper. Place a large heavy skillet over medium-high heat. Add the oil, and when hot, sear the steaks for about 5 to 6 minutes per side for medium-rare. Remove to a plate to rest.

Turn up the heat and add the mushrooms. Add the broth and use a wooden spoon to scrape the bottom of the pan. Once the broth has deglazed the caramelized meat juices from the bottom of the pan, add the butter and stir until it disappears. Turn up the heat and add the mushrooms mixture. Stir to combine. Taste and adjust seasoning.

Place the steaks on warm plates and spoon the warm mushrooms over the meat. Serve immediately.

chicken parmesan casserole with tomato sauce

Your dreams have been answered! Everyone's favorite Italian-style chicken dish is now available in casserole form.

serves 6

6 (6-7 ounce) boneless, skinless chicken breasts

Salt and freshly ground black pepper, to taste

2 Tbsp olive oil

2 cloves garlic, minced

4 cups marinara sauce

¼ cup chopped basil

1 cup (8 ounces) shredded mozzarella

½ cup (4 ounces) grated Parmesan

1 (5 ounce) package garlic croutons

For the marinara sauce

¼ cup olive oil

1 onion, diced

1 rib celery, finely dice

4 cloves garlic, minced

1 Tsp salt

2 Tsp sugar

½ Tsp dried Italian herbs

Pinch of red pepper flakes

1 Tsp anchovy paste

1 Tsp white wine vinegar

1 Tbsp tomato paste

2 (28 ounce) cans whole peeled plum tomatoes, coarsely pureed

2 Tbsp chopped fresh basil

Preheat oven to 350°F. Season the chicken breasts with salt and pepper. Set aside. Spread the olive oil, garlic, and red pepper flakes evenly on the bottom of a 9 x 13-inch casserole dish. Add 1 cup of the marinara sauce, and spread evenly. Place the chicken breasts in the dish, and space evenly. Top with the rest of the marinara sauce, basil and half the mozzarella and Parmesan cheeses. Sprinkle the croutons evenly over the chicken, then top with the remaining cheeses. Bake for 40 minutes, or until the top is browned and the chicken is cooked through. Let rest before serving.

To make the marinara sauce: In a saucepan, sauté the onions and celery in the olive oil for 5 to 6 minutes, or until translucent. Add the garlic and cook for 1 minute more. Add the salt, sugar, dried herbs, pepper flakes, anchovy paste, vinegar, and tomato paste. Cook, stirring, for 2 minutes. Add the tomatoes, bring to a simmer, turn down to low and simmer gently, stirring occasionally, for 45 minutes. Add water if necessary, to adjust thickness. Adjust the seasoning to taste, and reserve.

spaghetti and meatballs

Did you know that spaghetti and meatballs is an American invention? That's right, Italians don't believe in serving pasta and meatballs together. Hey, they don't know what they're missing!

makes 24 meatballs

2 tablespoons olive oil

1 yellow onion, diced

4 garlic cloves, minced

½ teaspoon dried Italian herbs

½ loaf day-old Italian bread, crust removed

¼ cup milk

2 pounds ground beef (recommend 80/20 lean/fat ratio)

2 teaspoons salt

1 teaspoon freshly ground black pepper

2 large eggs, beaten

¹/₃ cup chopped fresh Italian parsley

¾ cup freshly grated Parmigiano-Reggiano cheese, plus more for service

6 cups marinara sauce, or other prepared pasta sauce

1 cup water

Thick spaghetti (allow 4 ounces uncooked per person), cooked according to directions

Preheat oven to 425°F. Heat the olive oil in a saucepan over medium-low heat; add the onion, garlic, and a pinch of salt. Sauté for 6 to 7 minutes, or until soft and golden. Turn off heat, stir in the dried Italian herbs, let cool to room temperature.

Tear the bread into small chunks and place into a food processor (work in batches depending on the size of the machine). Pulse on and off to make fine breadcrumbs. You'll need 2 cups total. Add the crumbs to a bowl and toss with the milk to moisten. Let sit 10 minutes.

In a large mixing bowl, use your hands to combine the beef, salt, black pepper, eggs, parsley, cheese, breadcrumbs, and cooled onion mixture.

Wet your hands and roll golf ball-size meatballs; arrange on an oiled sheet pan. Bake the meatballs for 20 minutes. While the meatballs are browning in the oven, bring the pasta sauce and water to a simmer. When the meatballs are done, transfer into the hot sauce. Turn heat to very low, cover, and simmer gently for 45 minutes.

When they're done, cook the spaghetti, drain well (never rinse), and add to a large pasta bowl. Ladle some of the sauce over the pasta and toss to coat. Serve the spaghetti topped with the meatballs, sauce, and freshly grated Parmesan cheese.

slow-roasted pulled pork with kansas city barbeque sauce

The term "fork-tender" was invented for slow-roasted pork shoulder. Sure, it takes half a day to make, but the building anticipation makes that first bite into the sticky, succulent meat even more special.

serves 6-8

3½ to 4 pounds pork shoulder roast, also called pork butt or Boston butt

1 Tsp liquid smoke,

For the dry rub

2 Tbsp firmly packed dark brown sugar

1 Tbsp salt

1 Tbsp black pepper

1 Tbsp paprika

2 Tsp chile powder

2 Tsp garlic powder

2 Tsp onion powder

2 Tsp ground cumin

1 Tsp cayenne pepper

For the sauce

2 cups ketchup

²/₃ cup dark molasses

½ cup white vinegar

1 Tsp paprika

1 Tsp chili powder

1 Tsp hot sauce

½ Tsp black pepper

½ Tsp salt

½ Tsp ground cinnamon

½ Tsp ground allspice

½ Tsp ground mace

½ Tsp liquid smoke

Preheat oven to 215°F. Rinse the meat, and pat dry with paper towels. Trim off any large pieces of excess fat. Mix the rub ingredients together, and thoroughly coat all sides of the pork.

Place the pork, fattier side up, in a large Dutch oven. Pour ⅓ cup water into a small, ovenproof ramekin, and add the liquid smoke; place in the Dutch oven next to the meat. As the pork roasts, this will add moisture as well as a subtle smokiness to the meat. Cover tightly with the lid, and place in the center of the preheated oven. Roast for 12 hours, or until fork tender, or the internal temperature reaches 200°F. Turn off the oven and allow the pork to rest for 1 hour.

To serve, place the pork on a cutting board and using two forks, pull it apart into small pieces. (Some use a knife to chop the succulent meat, but legally you can no longer call it "pulled" pork.) Adjust the seasoning, and serve with the sauce.

For the sauce: Whisk together the ingredients in a saucepan. Bring to a simmer over medium-low heat. Cook, stirring, for 3 minutes. Remove from heat, and let cool to room temperature before serving.

'the best' grilled marinated flank steak

An easy overnight marinade is the secret to this delicious grilled flank steak. It's not called "the best" for nothing – get ready for some juicy, flavorful beef!

serves 4-6

4 cloves garlic, minced

¼ cup olive oil

¼ cup firmly packed brown sugar

2 tablespoons red wine vinegar

¼ cup soy sauce

1 teaspoon Dijon mustard

1 teaspoon freshly ground black pepper

1 whole trimmed flank steak (about 1½ to 2 pounds)

Salt to taste

Add all the ingredients, except the flank steak and salt, into a large, zip top freezer bag. Seal and shake to combine. Add the flank steak and reseal the bag, squeezing out most of the air. Refrigerate for at least 6 hours, but better overnight.

Remove the flank steak from the marinade to a large plate. The marinade can be poured in a small saucepan, boiled, and served with the cooked steak. Pat the flank steak dry with paper towels. Season both sides with salt and freshly ground black pepper to taste. Let sit out at room temperature for 15 minutes. Preheat your grill. Brush a little oil on the grates and place the steak on the grill.

Grill over high direct heat for 5 to 6 minutes per side for medium-rare, or until it reaches your desired degree of doneness. Transfer to a clean plate and loosely cover with foil. Let rest for 10 minutes before cutting into thin slices across the grain.

Note: This flank steak is best cooked over a hot charcoal fire, but it will also work on a gas grill, indoor grill pan, or broiler.

whole roast garlic herb chicken with pan gravy

The only thing better than a fragrant, beautifully browned roast chicken is one served with a rich, freshly made pan gravy. The keys to this great recipe are a very hot oven and using a roasting pan you can also make the sauce in after the chicken is cooked.

serves 4

1 large (about 5 pounds) whole chicken, rinsed, dried with paper towels

4 cloves garlic

1/3 cup olive oil

2 teaspoons minced fresh thyme leaves

2 teaspoons minced fresh rosemary leaves

1 teaspoon dried Italian herbs

Salt and freshly ground black pepper to taste

For the gravy

1½ tablespoons reserved chicken fat

1 tablespoon butter

1 tablespoon flour

2 cups cold chicken broth

½ teaspoon balsamic vinegar

4 sprigs fresh thyme

Salt and freshly ground black pepper to taste

Preheat oven to 450°F. Remove skins and crush the garlic cloves with the flat of a knife. Mince and and press until it is a very fine paste.

Add olive oil, garlic, thyme, rosemary and dried Italian herbs to a large mixing bowl. Rub the chicken inside and out with the mixture. Continue or leave to marinate overnight or for a few hours.

Place chicken in an ovenproof skillet or roasting pan. Season the cavity with salt and freshly ground black pepper. Truss the legs with kitchen string.

Place in the center of the oven and roast for one hour or until a thermometer registers 165°F. Remove the chicken, place on a platter and cover with foil. Allow to rest while making the gravy.

Pour the excess chicken fat from the pan, leaving 1½ tablespoons behind. Place back on the stove and add the butter. When the butter melts add a little flour and cook, stirring with a whisk constantly until golden brown. Whisk in 2 cups of cold chicken broth, balsamic vinegar, thyme, salt, and pepper to taste. Turn the heat to high, and boil for 5 minutes stirring until the gravy is thickened.

old-fashioned chicken and dumplings

This is one of America's ultimate comfort foods. Some folks like their dumplings light and airy, while others prefer them more hearty and dense. These are somewhere in between, but every bit as delicious.

serves 6

2 Tbsp vegetable oil

1 chicken (4 to 5 pounds), cut in quarters

1 quart chicken broth

3 cups water

4 cloves garlic, peeled

1 bay leaf

4 springs fresh thyme

5 Tbsp butter

2 carrots, cut into ½-inch pieces

2 ribs celery, cut into ½-inch pieces

1 large onion, chopped

5 tablespoons flour

1½ Tsp salt

Freshly ground black pepper to taste

Dash of hot sauce

For the dumplings

1¾ cups all-purpose flour

1 Tsp salt

2 Tsp baking powder

¼ teaspoon baking soda

3 Tbsp cold butter

2 Tbsp thinly sliced scallion tops

¼ cup buttermilk

¾ cup milk

Heat the oil in a Dutch oven on the stove over high heat. Brown the chicken pieces and add broth, water, garlic, bay leaf and thyme. Boil and then turn heat down and simmer covered for 30 minutes; then remove chicken to a bowl. Strain the cooking liquid into a separate bowl, skimming off any fat.

Place the Dutch oven over medium heat and add butter, carrots, celery and onion. Sauté for 5 minutes; stir in the flour. Cook for 2 minutes and then whisk in the reserved cooking liquid one cup at a time. Add salt, pepper, and hot sauce. Reduce the heat and simmer covered for 30 minutes until the vegetables are tender. Remove the chicken meat from the bones, tear into chunks, and add to the cooked vegetables.

To make the dumplings: Combine flour, salt, baking powder, and baking soda into a mixing bowl. Cut in the cold butter using a pastry blender until the mixture is coarse crumbs. Add the scallions, buttermilk, and milk and stir with a fork into a thick dough. Turn the heat under the Dutch oven to medium, and drop balls of the dumpling dough into the pot. Cover and cook for 15 minutes or until the dumplings are cooked in the middle.

roast turkey breast with cranberry sauce

By taking the breast off the bone, you'll get an easier to cook roast, and a much prettier presentation. Any fresh herbs from the garden work beautifully in this recipe.

serves 4

1 (3 pound) boned turkey breast

For the herb rub

2 tablespoons soft butter

2 tablespoons olive oil

1 teaspoon lemon juice

1 garlic clove, finely minced

1 tablespoon chopped fresh parsley

1 teaspoon chopped fresh thyme leaves

1 teaspoon chopped fresh rosemary leaves

¼ teaspoon dried sage, or poultry seasoning

Salt and freshly ground black pepper to taste

For the sauce

1 pound fresh or thawed frozen cranberries

1 tablespoon grated orange zest

²/₃ cup freshly squeezed orange juice

½ cup light brown sugar

¼ cup sugar

²/₃ cup water

Preheat oven to 425°F. Add the herb rub ingredients to a small bowl, and whisk to combine. Place the breast, skin side down, on the cutting board. Fold the tenderloin toward the thinner side of the breast. Using a boning knife, make a slice into the thickest part of the breast, creating a shallow flap. Be careful not to cut all the way through. Season very generously with salt and pepper. Rub on the herb spread. Fold the tenderloin back over into the center of the breast and gather together.

With kitchen twine, tie a square knot around the breast at the thickest point. Repeat every inch until the breast is trussed into a round, tight package. Flip over, skin side up, and place in a lightly oiled shallow roasting pan. Rub any leftover herb rub over the skin, and season with salt and pepper to taste.

Roast the turkey for 20 minutes, then reduce the heat to 325°F. and continue roasting until a thermometer registers 165°F. when inserted into the thickest area of the breast (about 45 minutes). Cover loosely with foil and let rest for 15 minutes before serving. Serve with cranberry sauce.

For the sauce: Put the cranberries in a heavy-bottom pan with the orange zest and juice, sugars, and water. Bring to a boil, then reduce the heat and simmer for 12 to 15 minutes, until the cranberries have burst. Remove from the heat. Allow to cool. Serve chilled or at room temperature.

chicken fried steak with country cream gravy

You can use other cuts of beef, like round steak, for this recipe, but the nooks and crannies that the cube steak provides make it ideal for this truck stop classic.

serves 4

4 (6 oz) beef cube steaks

Salt and freshly ground black pepper to taste

1 cup all-purpose flour

1 tbsp paprika

½ tsp white pepper

2 eggs, beaten

¼ cup milk

Vegetable oil as needed

For the gravy

4 oz ground pork sausage, or pork sausage link with casing removed

3 green onions, light parts chopped, green parts sliced and reserved

3 tbsps butter

¼ cup all-purpose flour

2½ cups cold milk

Salt and freshly ground black pepper to taste

Pinch of cayenne

Season both sides of the cube steaks generously with salt and pepper. Whisk together the eggs and milk in a pie pan and reserve. Add the flour, paprika, and white pepper into a second pie pan, and mix well to combine.

Dip the cube steaks into the egg mixture and then dredge in flour, coating both sides. Place the egged and floured steaks on a plate, and allow to rest for 10 minutes.

Add about a ¼ inch of vegetable oil to a large skillet, and place over medium-high heat. When the oil begins to shimmer, add the steaks and cook about 3 to 4 minutes per side, until golden brown and cooked through. Remove and drain for a couple minutes on a wire rack set over some paper towels. If working in batches, keep the cooked steaks in a warm oven until the rest are done.

Gravy: Lightly brown the sausage in a medium saucepan over medium heat. As it cooks, break the meat up into very small pieces with a wooden spoon. Add the light parts of the green onion and the butter; sauté for a few minutes, until the onions are translucent.

Stir in the flour and cook for 3 minutes. Whisk in the cold milk until combined. Simmer and reduce the heat, stirring until thickened. Season with salt, pepper and cayenne to taste.

broiled rainbow trout with lemon parsley brown butter

One of the simplest of all seafood accompaniments, this classic brown butter sauce is perfect with mild-flavored trout.

serves 6

6 tablespoons unsalted butter

6 whole boneless rainbow trout

Salt and freshly ground black pepper to taste

3 tablespoons fresh lemon juice

¼ cup chopped fresh parsley

Lemon wedges to garnish

Place the butter in a saucepan over medium-low heat. Cook until the butter turns a golden brown color, and takes on a nutty aroma. Reduce heat to very low and keep warm.

Remove the heads from the trout, and place skin-side-down on lightly-greased foil-lined baking sheets. Lightly brush a little of the browned butter over the surface. Season generously with salt and fresh ground black pepper.

Broil about 4 inches from the flame for 3 to 5 minutes, or until fish flakes when tested with a fork. While the fish is cooking, turn the butter up to medium heat and whisk in the lemon juice. As soon as the mixture comes to a boil, add the parsley, turn off the heat.

When ready, serve the trout on warm plates with the hot lemon parsley brown butter spooned over the top. Serve lemon wedges on the side.

scrumptious treats

double fudge brownies

If you like dry, cake-like brownies, this recipe isn't for you.
These are moist, fudgy, and very chocolaty.

makes 9 brownies

1½ cups (8 ounces) bittersweet baking chocolate, broken or chopped into small pieces

⅓ cup butter, sliced into pieces

1 cup sugar

¼ teaspoon salt

2 tablespoons water

2 large eggs

1 teaspoon vanilla extract

¾ cup all-purpose flour

½ cup chopped walnuts (optional)

Preheat oven to 325°F. Place the chocolate, butter, sugar, salt, and water in small saucepan over a very low flame. Heat, stirring often, until the chocolate and butter are melted.

Pour into a mixing bowl. Stir in the eggs, one at a time. Stir in the vanilla extract. Stir in the flour. Stir in the nuts, if using.

Pour into a lightly greased 8 inch-square baking dish.

Bake for 35 minutes. Cool completely before cutting into 9 squares.

cinnamon swirl sour cream bundt cake

The word "Coffee" is not part of the title of this recipe, but make no mistake, this is a coffee cake. In fact, if you don't drink coffee, please start before attempting this moist, spicy cake.

serves 6-8

2½ cups all-purpose flour

1 teaspoon baking powder

1 teaspoon baking soda

½ teaspoon salt

¾ cup (1½ sticks) unsalted butter

1½ cups sugar

3 large eggs

1 cup sour cream

1 teaspoon vanilla extract

½ cup chopped walnuts, optional

For the swirl

1 tablespoon ground cinnamon

3 tablespoons firmly packed light brown sugar

2 tablespoons sugar

For the glaze

1 cup confectioners' sugar

1½ tablespoons milk

1 teaspoon ground cinnamon, or to taste

Preheat oven to 350°F. Whisk together the flour, baking powder, baking soda, and salt in a mixing bowl for a minute; reserve until needed.

Cream the butter and sugar together until light and fluffy. Beat in the eggs one at a time, mixing thoroughly before adding the next. Beat in the sour cream and vanilla extract until combined. Add the flour mixture, stirring just until combined. Stir in the walnuts.

Butter a 10-inch Bundt pan, and lightly dust with flour. Pour half the batter into the pan and spread evenly. Mix the ingredients for the swirl in a small bowl. Sprinkle evenly around the center of the batter. Cover with the rest of the batter.

Bake for 50 minutes, or until a tester inserted in the center comes out clean. Let cool 20 minutes before removing from the pan.

For the glaze: Add the confectioners' sugar to a small mixing bowl, stir in enough milk to create a thick, but pourable glaze. Stir in the cinnamon to taste. Drizzle over the top of the cake. Once the icing is set, slice and serve with lots of hot coffee.

carrot cake with cream cheese frosting

If someone created a list of the greatest cake/frosting combinations of all time, this dense, moist carrot cake topped with cream cheese frosting has to be at the top.

serves 8

2 cups all-purpose flour

1 teaspoon salt

2 teaspoons baking powder

1 teaspoon baking soda

2 teaspoons cinnamon

½ teaspoon ground ginger

2 cups sugar

1¼ cups vegetable oil

4 large eggs

¼ cup melted butter

2 cups grated carrots

1 (8-ounce) can crushed pineapple, drained

½ cup chopped pecans

½ cup chopped walnuts

For the frosting

½ cup unsalted butter, softened

1 cup (8 ounce) cream cheese, softened

1 tablespoon milk

1 teaspoon vanilla

1 pound confectioners' sugar

Preheat oven to 350°F. Whisk together the flour, salt, baking powder, baking soda, cinnamon, and ginger in a mixing bowl for a minute or two; reserve until needed.

In another mixing bowl, combine the sugar, oil, and eggs. Whisk until thoroughly combined. Whisk in the melted butter. Use a spatula to stir in the carrots, pineapple, and nuts. Stir in the flour mixture in two additions.

Scrape the batter into a lightly greased 13x9-inch cake pan. Bake for about 40 minutes, or until the top springs back slightly when gently touched with your finger. Remove and allow to cool completely before frosting.

To make the frosting: Using an electric mixer, beat together the butter, cream cheese, milk, and vanilla until light and fluffy. Gradually beat in the confectioners' sugar to form a smooth frosting. Spread evenly over the cooled cake.

whoopie pies

You have to love any recipe whose name comes from such a joyous exclamation! "Whoopie!" indeed.

makes 8-10

2 cups all-purpose flour

3 tablespoons unsweetened cocoa powder

½ teaspoon baking soda

¼ teaspoon salt

½ cup (1 stick) unsalted butter, softened

1 cup firmly packed dark brown sugar

1 large egg

1¼ teaspoons vanilla

½ cup buttermilk

For the filling

4 ounces softened cream cheese

1 (7-ounce) jar marshmallow crème

Preheat oven to 375°F. Add the flour, cocoa powder, baking soda and salt to a mixing bowl. Stir the mixture with a whisk to combine and aerate. Reserve until needed.

Cream the butter and brown sugar in a large mixing bowl, with an electric mixer until light and fluffy. Beat in the egg and vanilla until thoroughly combined. Add a third of the flour mixture; stir until combined. Add half the buttermilk; stir until combined. Add half the remaining flour; stir until combined. Add the remaining buttermilk, stir in, and finally mix in the last of the flour.

Line two heavy-duty baking sheets with silicon baking mats or parchment paper. Spoon the batter on the baking sheets, forming rounds about ½-inch high and 3-inches wide. (You can make these as small or large as you like; the most important thing is they all remain the same size, so they bake evenly.)

Bake for 12 to 14 minutes, or until the tops are slightly firm to the touch. Remove and let rest for 15 minutes on the baking sheets. Remove to racks and let cool completely before filling.

To make the filling: In a mixing bowl beat the cream cheese until light and fluffy. Fold in the marshmallow crème. Spread a couple spoonfuls of filling on the flat side of one of the cakes, and top with another to form a sandwich.

butterscotch blondies

Bored with brownies? What better alternative than
moist and tender butterscotch blondies?

makes 9 blondies

1 cup all-purpose flour

1/8 teaspoon baking soda

1/2 teaspoon baking powder

1/4 teaspoon salt

1/2 cup (1 stick) butter, melted

3/4 cup firmly packed light brown sugar

1/4 cup sugar

1 large egg plus 1 egg yolk, beaten together

1 teaspoon vanilla extract

1/2 cup butterscotch chips

1/4 cup milk chocolate chips

1/4 cup chopped dry-roasted cashews

Preheat oven to 350°F. In a large bowl combine the flour, baking soda, baking powder, and salt to a mixing bowl. Stir with a whisk to combine. Reserve.

In another large mixing bowl, whisk together the melted butter and sugars until combined. Add the eggs and vanilla, and stir to combine. Switch to a wooden spoon and stir in the flour mixture. Fold in the butterscotch chips, chocolate chips, and cashews.

With a spatula, scrape the batter into a lightly greased 8x8-inch pan or glass baking dish. Smooth to distribute evenly. Bake for about 35 minutes, or until the top is golden brown and a tester inserted in the center comes out clean.

Cool before cutting into 9 bars.

boston cream pie

Sure you can make this cake from scratch, but let's face it, in this classic American dessert the cake is nothing more than a chocolate and pastry cream delivery system.

serves 6-8

1 (18.25 ounce) package white or yellow cake mix, prepared according to directions and cooled

For the pastry cream

7 tablespoons sugar

2 tablespoons cornstarch

3 large eggs

1 cup whipping cream

1 cup whole milk

1 tablespoon butter

1½ teaspoons vanilla extract

Pinch of salt

For the chocolate topping (called a ganache)

4 ounces high-quality bittersweet chocolate, chopped

½ cup heavy cream

1 teaspoon butter

For the pastry cream: Combine the sugar, cornstarch, and eggs in a mixing bowl; whisk vigorously until the mixture is light and creamy; set aside.

Bring the cream, milk, and butter to a boil in a small saucepan over medium-high heat. Quickly whisk in the egg mixture, and boil, stirring constantly, for exactly one minute. The mixture should become very thick, very quickly. Remove from heat and strain into a bowl. Cover the surface with plastic wrap, and let cool at room temperature for 20 minutes, then refrigerate until completely cold; overnight is best. Before completing the cake, whisk in the vanilla extract, and a pinch of salt.

When your pastry cream is ready, and your cakes have been baked and completely cooled, you're ready to assemble. Place one layer down on a cake plate, top with the pastry cream and lay the other cake gently on top. If you want less cake you can just use one layer, sliced through the center to make two thinner layers.

For the chocolate topping: Place the chocolate in a heat-proof bowl and set aside. Bring the cream and butter to a simmer over medium-high heat, then quickly pour over the chocolate. Let sit for 3 minutes, then gently whisk to combine. When the mixture has thickened slightly, yet is still thin enough to pour, spread evenly over the top of the cake. Refrigerate until the chocolate has firmed up completely before slicing and serving.

pound cake with orange glaze

Perfect with a cup of tea or coffee, this simple pound cake
is also great sitting under some fresh fruit.

serves 6

2 cups all-purpose flour

1 teaspoon baking powder

¼ teaspoon baking soda

½ teaspoon salt

1 cup (2 sticks) unsalted butter

1¼ cups sugar

1 tablespoon grated lemon zest

1 tablespoon grated orange zest

4 eggs

½ cup buttermilk

1 teaspoon vanilla extract

For the glaze

1 cup confectioners' sugar

1½ tablespoons fresh orange juice, or as needed

1 tablespoon freshly grated orange zest

Preheat oven to 325°F. Butter one loaf pan, and dust with flour. Set aside.

Sift together the flour, baking powder, baking soda, and salt in a mixing bowl. Set aside.

In a large mixing bowl, use an electric mixer to cream the butter, sugar, and zests until very light and creamy. Beat in the eggs, one at time, beating very thoroughly after each addition. Use a spatula to mix in flour alternately with the buttermilk, ending with flour. Add the vanilla extract. Scrape the batter into the prepared loaf pan.

Bake for 1 hour to 1 hour 15 minutes, or until a tester inserted in the center comes out clean. Remove and let rest for 15 minutes, then turn onto a cooling rack. Let cool 15 more minutes before glazing.

To make the glaze: Stir together the glaze ingredients, adding enough orange juice to get a smooth spreadable consistency. Apply to the top of the warm cake. Let the pound cake cool completely before slicing.

red velvet cake

This is one of the few recipes where it's completely acceptable, if not mandatory, to use food coloring. Some older recipes actually call for beets to give this southern staple its signature color. As delicious as a "beet-infused cake" sounds, we'll just stick with a natural red dye.

serves 12

1 cup (2 sticks) unsalted butter, plus extra for greasing

4 tablespoon water

½ cup unsweetened cocoa

3 eggs

1 cup buttermilk

2 teaspoons vanilla extract

2 tablespoons red food coloring

2½ cups all-purpose flour

½ cup cornstarch

1½ teaspoons baking powder

1½ cups sugar

For the frosting

1 cup (8 ounces) cream cheese

3 tablespoons unsalted butter

3 tablespoons sugar

1 teaspoon vanilla extract

Preheat oven to 375°F. Grease two 9-inch layer cake pans and line the bottoms with parchment paper.

Place the butter, water, and cocoa in a small saucepan and heat gently, without boiling, stirring until the butter is melted and the mixture is smooth. Remove from the heat and let cool slightly.

Beat together the eggs, buttermilk, vanilla extract, and food coloring until frothy. Beat in the butter mixture. Sift together the flour, cornstarch, and baking powder, then stir quickly and evenly into the mixture with the sugar.

Divide the batter between the prepared pans and bake for 25 to 30 minutes, or until risen and firm to the touch. Cool in the pans for 3 to 4 minutes, then turn out and finish cooling on a wire rack.

For the frosting: Beat together all the ingredients until smooth. Use about half of the frosting to sandwich the cakes together, then spread the remainder over the top, swirling with a metal spatula.

double chocolate muffins

Chocolate/chocolate muffins—perfect for breakfast, a
snack, or even dessert! Perfection!

makes 8 muffins

¾ cup self-rising flour

½ cup cocoa powder

½ cup (1 stick) butter,
softened

½ cup sugar

2 large eggs

½ cup semisweet
chocolate chips

Preheat the oven to 375°F. Line a 12-cup muffin tin with
8 paper baking liners.

In a bowl, sift together the flour and cocoa powder.

In a large mixing bowl, beat together the butter, sugar, and
eggs until smooth.

Add half the dry ingredients and stir until combined; add
the remaining dry ingredients. Fold in the chocolate chips
until combined.

Spoon the batter into the prepared muffin cups.

Bake in the preheated oven for 20 to 25 minutes, or until
well risen and springy to the touch. Transfer to a wire rack
to cool completely.

index

deviled eggs 8
double chocolate muffins 92

eggs
  baked spinach and feta omelet 34
  deviled eggs 8
  eggs benedict 40
  new orleans-style french toast 36
  sausage and mushroom breakfast casserole 42

firehouse chili con carne 48
fish & seafood
  broiled rainbow trout with lemon parsley butter 72
  maryland crab cakes with tartar sauce 10
  potato pancakes with smoked salmon and dill sour
    cream 32

garden vegetable soup 22

maryland crab cakes with tartar sauce 10
mom's chicken noodle soup 20
mushrooms
  all-american meatloaf 52
  new york strip steak and mushrooms 54
  sausage and mushroom breakfast casserole 42

new orleans-style french toast 36
new york strip steak and mushrooms 54
nuts
  banana nut bread 44
  butterscotch blondies 84
  carrot cake with cream cheese frosting 80
  cinnamon swirl sour cream bundt cake 78
  double fudge brownies 74

pasta & noodles
  deli-style macaroni salad 24
  mom's chicken noodle soup 20
  spaghetti and meatballs 58
pineapple: carrot cake with cream cheese frosting 80
pork: slow-roasted pulled pork with kansas city
  barbeque sauce 60
potatoes
  corned beef hash 30
  potato pancakes with smoked salmon and dill sour
    cream 32
  sausage and mushroom breakfast casserole 42

pound cake with orange glaze 88

red velvet cake 90

salmon: potato pancakes with smoked salmon and
  dill sour cream 32
sausage
  chicken fried steak with country cream gravy 70
  chorizo and cheese quesadillas with chipotle sour
    cream 16
  sausage and mushroom breakfast casserole 42
spaghetti and meatballs 58
spinach
  baked spinach and feta omelet 34
  garden vegetable soup 22
  hot spinach and artichoke dip 14

tomatoes
  chicken parmesan casserole with tomato sauce 56
  corned beef hash 30
  firehouse chili con carne 48
  garden vegetable soup 22
  spaghetti and meatballs 58
tortillas: chorizo and cheese quesadillas with chipotle
  sour cream 16
trout: broiled rainbow trout with lemon parsley
  butter 72
turkey: roast turkey breast with cranberry sauce 68

walnuts
  banana nut bread 44
  carrot cake with cream cheese frosting 80
  cinnamon swirl sour cream bundt cake 78
  double fudge brownies 76
whoopie pies 82